Want to get promoted?

WANT TO GET PROMOTED?

Learn expert tips and Advice on how to get a job promotion in your work place

James Armstrong

Want to get promoted?

TABLE OF CONTENTS

INTRODUCTION

EXPERT TIPS AND ADVICE ON HOW TO GET A JOB PROMOTION IN YOUR WORK PLACE

#1) Good Job Record

#2) Punctuality to work

#3) A good team player:

#4) Be Ready Always:

#5) Get along with your colleagues and Get Noticed

#6) Scale Up your Qualification:

#7) Visit Various Listings For Open Jobs

Want to get promoted?

#8) Discuss with your boss.

HOW TO PREPARE FOR A JOB PROMOTION IN YOUR WORK PLACE

Prepare for an interview for the promotion

Get references from your superiors

Send a thank-you note

Spare out some time to say goodbye

Want to get promoted?

DEDICATION

I want to first of all dedicate this book to GOD almighty, without whom there will be no life.

This book is also dedicated to all sincere and hardworking youths all over the world.

Want to get promoted?

ACKNOWLEDGEMENT

I wish to always acknowledge my mother, Lady Catherine A. I can barely find the words to express all the wisdom, love and support you've given me. You are my number one fan and for that I am eternally grateful. If I am blessed to live long enough, I hope I will be as good a father to Alexander as you are and always have been to me. I Love You Mommy.

INTRODUCTION

Do you really want to get a promotion in your office?

Of course, Yes! Who wouldn't want that?

But what will you do if you are fascinated in getting a promotion but your manager does not seem to automatically offer you a new position?

Well, there are ways to request a promotion cautiously and increase your chances for the promotion.

So I suggest you read this manual to the end so you won't get to miss anything.

Want to get promoted?

Want to get promoted?

EXPERT TIPS AND ADVICE ON HOW TO GET A JOB PROMOTION IN YOUR WORK PLACE

Before I go further into this book, please take note of this – **make sure you are doing the right thing so as to get a positive reply.**

What are the right things I should do you may ask?

Well, these are the things that employers consider when evaluating employees to promote to a new position:

Want to get promoted?

#1) Good Job Record

The way you discharge your duties in your present position will be very important when you are being considered for a promotion. Excellent performance evaluations and your reputation as a standard employee usually carry a lot of weight when a company makes decisions about its staffing promotion.

#2) Punctuality to work

Always come on time to work and do not take more time off than you were assigned. If the manager notice that you're not serious with your job and sees you as someone who comes late always and as someone misses work more often than usual, it is going to be too bad and will definitely ruin your reputation and chances of being promoted.

#3) A good team player:

Always volunteer to assist with new projects in your work place. Also volunteer for committees or working groups. Offer to assist your boss and co-workers when time permits. Through this little act of kindness, you will be known as a good team player and as someone with whom colleagues would always want to work with.

#4) Be Ready Always:

In some cases, your employer may likely recognize your exceptional qualities and offer you a promotion. Of course, it is much easier when it turns out this way. But for some jobs and in some companies, you may need to request for a promotion before it can be given to you. Note that you may have to request or apply for the promotion you want before it can be offered to you.

#5) Get along with your colleagues and Get Noticed

Be present at company parties and meetings. The more close and connected you are with your colleagues, the more they are likely to know about you and the more you will stand out when the time comes for your promotion consideration. Managers are more likely to promote an employee they know too well than a random candidate they do not know much about.

#6) Scale Up your Qualification:

When your company offers opportunities for professional development classes, take advantage of all that you can. If your skills need to be updated and enhanced, take continuing education or college classes. In this way, your skills will be at the top level.

#7) Visit Various Listings For Open Jobs

Most big companies and smaller companies alike post job offers on their websites. Some positions may be open to internal candidates before being available to outside applicants, so you will have to jump in the competition. Check regularly for new lists and apply for jobs that fit well with your educational background, qualification and experience.

Want to get promoted?

#8) Discuss with your boss.

Be sure to inform your boss that you have interest in a new position. You will want him on your team because your references will be reviewed. It is not a good idea to keep it a top secret because your boss will surely find out about it. It is best that he hear it from you than from any one else. Offer to assist with the transition if you are chosen for a promotion.

HOW TO PREPARE FOR A JOB PROMOTION IN YOUR WORK PLACE

Step one:

Adhere to the submission guideline

Never assume you are going to get the promotion. The company may have other external candidates as well as other employees who might be interested in that position. Also, do not assume that the human resource manager or department manager reviewing your documents know your work experience. Take time to update

Want to get promoted?

your resume and write a specific cover letter for the position that interests you. Follow the normal application process, know if there is a formal procedure to apply for the position you're vying for.

Want to get promoted?

Step two:

Prepare for an interview for the promotion

If you applied or you're being considered for a new position in your company for a promotion, you may be interviewed for the position you're interested in. So you have to be prepared for an opportunity to move up in your career ladder.

Want to get promoted?

Step three:

Get references from your superiors

Ask for a letter of recommendation from your supervisor and other managers with whom you have worked before now. References, especially of high-level personnel, carry a lot of weight.

Step four:

Send a thank-you note

Send a thank-you note or a thank-you email to all the people who interviewed you so as to reiterate your interest in the position.

Want to get promoted?

Step five:

Spare out some time to say goodbye

If all goes well and you were finally offered the promotion, take the time out to say goodbye to your former colleges and let them know that you will stay in touch. But you have to wait until the company formally announces your promotion to the new position before you can tell them about it. It is very important that the company first of all make the announcement first before you let your colleagues know about it and then finally say a goodbye to them.

Want to get promoted?

And that's the end!

Thanks for reading

Want to get promoted?

www.ingramcontent.com/pod-product-compliance
Lightning Source LLC
Chambersburg PA
CBHW031601210526
45464CB00003B/1374